Joseph
and the
Hidden Cup

To Megan

First published in Great Britain in 2018

Society for Promoting Christian Knowledge
36 Causton Street, London SW1P 4ST
www.spck.org.uk

Text copyright © Fiona Veitch Smith 2018
Illustrations copyright © Andy Catling 2018

British Library Cataloguing-in-Publication Data
A catalogue record for this book is available from the British Library

ISBN 978-0-281-07474-7

1 3 5 7 9 10 8 6 4 2

Typeset by Gill McLean
Printed in Great Britain by Ashford Colour Press

Produced on paper from sustainable forests

Joseph
and the
Hidden Cup

Fiona Veitch Smith

Illustrated by
Andy Catling

SPCK

Joseph was one of **twelve brothers** who used to live with their **dad** and **stepmothers** on a farm in the land of **Canaan**.

On the farm were sheep, goats
and *lots* and **lots** of cows.
There were **fat** cows and skinny cows
and **somewhere-in-between** cows,
but **Joseph** loved them *all.*

Now, **Joseph** no longer lived in **Canaan**.

His **brothers** were **jealous** of him

because their father had given him a **rainbow robe**.

Then they were *very* unkind and sold him as a **slave**.

The **slave traders** had taken him to Egypt where, eventually, he was set **free**

and was now the **second** most important person in the land.

There had been a **terrible** drought in Canaan, and there was **no food**, so Joseph's brothers had gone to Egypt to buy supplies.

They did not realize that the **person in *charge*** of all the **food** was **Joseph**.

Joseph was **still angry** with them.

He put **one** of the **brothers**, Simeon, in **prison** and sent the others home.

Back on the **farm**
things were *very* **bad**.
When the food from Egypt ran out,
the *whole* family – and
all the **animals** –
began to **starve**.

They were **SOOOOOO** hungry!

They wanted to go back to Egypt to buy *more* food.

The only problem was, **the person in charge** had said they **must** bring their **youngest brother Benjamin** with them, but their father didn't want to let him go.

When **Jacob** could hear
his children's **tummies grumble**, however,
he finally agreed to let them **leave**.

In Egypt, Joseph was **so** excited to see his brothers that he held an **enormous** dinner in their honour.

Simeon was **released** from prison
and Benjamin was given **five times more** food
than anyone else.

That was just as well because he was
the **greediest** boy in the family.

The **brothers** had brought **lots of presents** with them
and gave them all to **Joseph**,
but they *still didn't know* he was really their **brother**.

They had also brought **twice as much money**
as before to pay for the food . . .

because, last time, Joseph had told his guards to **put the money** *back* in the **brothers'** sacks.

The **boys** were **worried** that the Egyptians would think they had **stolen** it,

so they gave it back to them again.

As the **brothers** were **packing** their **donkeys** to leave, Joseph – who still had **not forgiven them** for selling him as a **slave** –

told his **helpers** to hide his **special silver cup** in **Benjamin's** sack.

The **brothers** did **not know a _thing_** about it.
They **happily** waved goodbye
to the **Egyptians**

and headed home to **Canaan.**

When the **brothers** were only
a short way
into their journey,

Joseph sent his soldiers charging after them.

The **captain of the guard** forced the **brothers** to stop
and said, 'Someone has **stolen** our **lord's** silver cup!
He thinks you are **thieves!** Now *open* your sacks!'

'**Thieves?**' asked Judah, the fourth-eldest **brother**.
'We would *never* **steal** anything!
Search us and if you find what you're looking for,
the **thief** will become **your master's slave**.'

So the soldiers **searched** the brothers' sacks, **one by one.**

Then, as they *knew* they would, they **found** the silver cup in Benjamin's things.

'It **wasn't** me!' cried Benjamin. 'I didn't steal it!'

But the **soldiers** wouldn't listen
and took all the **brothers** **back** to Joseph in **Egypt**.

Joseph was looking **very** stern.
'How **dare** you **steal** from me!' he said,

'The **thief** must now be my **slave**.

Take him away!'

Joseph told the guards
to put Benjamin in **chains**,
but **Judah** would not let him go.

He **threw** himself at Joseph's feet and begged,
'Please, sir, *don't* take him. Take **me** instead.
Our **father** has already lost **one son** –
a **boy** called Joseph – and if
he loses **Benjamin** as well,
he will **die** of sadness.'

When **Joseph** heard this, his **own heart broke**.
All **anger** was gone.
It was time to **forgive** his brothers
for what they had done to him.
'**Let Benjamin go**,' he said to the **guards**.
Then he said to his **brothers**,

'**I am Joseph** – the **one** you thought was **dead**.'
Then he took off his **Egyptian** headdress
and showed his **brothers** who **he really** was.

Joseph's brothers couldn't believe it!
They were all **so happy**.
There were lots of **hugs** and kisses
and **brothers** saying **sorry** to brothers.

Then, after they'd had a **huge party** to celebrate,
they all went home
to tell their **father**, Jacob, the **good news**.

Jacob was the **happiest** man in the world.
Finally, he had all **twelve** of his **sons together**.

Jacob gave Joseph back his **rainbow robe**
that he'd kept for so many years.

Then **Pharaoh** gave the family **new land** to farm in **Egypt**.
Whenever he could, **Joseph** came to visit.

On the farm were sheep, goats and
lots and **lots** of **brothers**.

Joseph loved them **all**.

Also available in the Young Joseph series

Joseph and the Rainbow Robe
978-0-281-07468-6

Joseph and the Jealous Brothers
978-0-281-07469-3

Joseph and the Lying Lady
978-0-281-07470-9

Joseph and the Forgetful Servant
978-0-281-07471-6

Joseph and the Dreaming Pharaoh
978-0-281-07472-3

Joseph and the Fearful Family
978-0-281-07473-0